I Held The Flag Today

Words Of Patriotism

By

Jerry Plantz
The Patriotic Poet

ISBN: 1-4107-6714-0 (e-book)
ISBN: 1-4107-6713-2 (Paperback)

This book is printed on acid free paper.

Email: poetusa@swbell.net
Website: www.thepatrioticpoet.com

1stBooks - rev. 08/29/03

Steve

Best wishes

Jerry Glanty

ABOUT THE AUTHOR

JERRY PLANTZ

Jerry Plantz was born in Pittsburgh, Pennsylvania, received his B.A. from Duquesne University, is an Army veteran and a former award winning television executive news producer. His extensive communications background includes print and broadcast reporting as well as being a columnist, magazine publisher, copywriter, speech writer, public relations and marketing consultant, and video producer. Many of his popular patriotic poems, such as "I Held The Flag Today," "There's A Memorial In Kansas City," and "I Watched Them Go," were published separately in newspapers, magazines and the Internet and read at national memorial sites. This patriotic poet, who has received various awards and citations including, Humanitarian of the Year, resides in Lee's Summit, Missouri.

To our military throughout the globe.

To those beneath the tombstones, flowers and flags.

ACKNOWLEDGMENTS

One seldom achieves goals without the assistance and input of a friendly hand or an objective mind. It is with deep pride that I acknowledge, some of the many, who have made this book possible.

To my friend Carlyn Jurgensmeyer who was my confidante and second pair of eyes for searching out imperfections, of which there were many. Her common sense and unshakable beliefs have been an inspiration to me. And to her parents who were often the only focus study group to test my wares.

To Sister Mary Janet Ryan, my grade school teacher and lifelong mentor, for keeping me after school to learn fractions and for being the pillar of strength for me in moments of triumph, or in deep sorrow. You have meant so much to generations of pupils that you have taught.

To Ted Dorfman, the owner of the Great American Flag, for inviting a stranger to come to Jennerstown, Pennsylvania on September 24, 2001 and to recite his poem "I Held The Flag Today" during a special 9/11 candle light ceremony just 15 miles from the crash site of United Flight 93.

To David White and his staff of The National Flag Foundation for publishing my poem in their national quarterly magazine and for providing me with a platform from which to present my work.

To Bob Lewellen, commissioner of the Kansas City, Missouri Parks and Recreation Board and The Native Sons of Kansas City, Missouri, for promoting "There's A Memorial In Kansas City," and for recommending that the poem be recited at the rededication ceremonies of the World War One Liberty Memorial on May 25, 2002.

To the city of Lee's Summit, The VFW and The American Legion.

To Steve White, friend and author, for his advice and input.

To Tom Zart, The talented Westport Poet, who says I'm his favorite poet.

To my long time friend and talented hair stylist Jonnie Pickering and her husband Ken who always supported me in all of my endeavors, especially my poetry.

To my family and relatives who through the years remained true to the axiom that - a family that gets together at every holiday and special occasion and plays cards together, stays together.

To my cat Troubles, who had the wisdom to often get me up at three in the morning to be let out.
He knew it was difficult for me to go back to sleep so I began writing. My buddy of 15 years passed away on April 2, 2002. To a new cat named Hohnee who is following in his brother's paw prints.

Thanks, to all of you.

INTRODUCTION

I never set out to write a book of patriotic poems. September 11 made that decision for me.

Every American can recall when and where they were on that horrific morning in 2001 when another day of infamy was recorded in our inexorable flow of history. The events of 2001 affected all of our lives. Just how significantly became evident for me on Sunday morning September 15 at 8:00 a.m. when I raised the flag at my home, which I had been faithfully performing since September 11. That day shattered my mundane writing of an intended screenplay and directed me down a new path of unrelenting determination. It was a day that I met a friend. An unswerving and unfailing friend known as "I Held The Flag Today." For days I wanted to write something that would soothe my spirit and pay homage to those who died that day. Amid an avalanche of news and information about that tragic event I was trying to determine what really binds all of us as Americans. Many characteristics came to mind: our indomitable spirit, our perseverance, our diversity, our melting pot. Still, the question remained, what is it that makes us all think as one, cry as one and die as one? Then, while literally holding the flag as I displayed it that Sunday morning, it came to me. The unity was in my hands - The Stars Spangled Banner.

I immediately went to my computer and the story line and the words came spewing out. Perhaps, the inspiration came from my assisting in military funerals while serving in the Army in the late Fifties, or the thought of all of the military funerals that soon were to be. I began - I held the flag today, it's been awhile and it's not my style but I touched it where it lay. Suddenly It was the start of a story. I kept writing, until several hours later, the first and second drafts were finished. I don't even remember how I came up with the story line for it has nothing to do with my father or family. However, it is indeed the sad experience of millions of Americans.

The final one line ending, "Are you guys ready? Let's roll!" breaks meter and rhyme. I was probably the first author in the nation to write of the significance of Todd Beamer's rallying cry on United Flight 93. To me it was the Minutemen crossing the Delaware River on Christmas Day, The Rough Riders storming San Juan Hill, the Dough Boys racing forward at Verdun, General Jimmy Doolittle's daring raid on Japan, our soldiers taking Pork Chop Hill, our troops moving through the jungles of Vietnam, an armada of tanks and troops rolling across the Iraqi desert, John Adams addressing the Continental Congress, the cry of dreamers as they boarded their Conestoga wagons heading West, and of course, those brave heroes on that doomed plane as they stormed the cockpit. It was a line that just had to be part of the poem.

I had no plans for the poem other than to place it in my book of unpublished material. Then I read on the Internet on September 17 that a seven-ton flag was to be unfurled near the crash site of United Flight 93 during a candlelight tribute and ceremony on Monday, September 24. It was the Great American Flag, which the Kansas Cosmosphere and Space Center in Hutchinson, Kansas had sold to Ted Dorfman, an Army veteran who lived in Greensburg, Pa. which is east of Pittsburgh, Pa. my native hometown. I tracked down the reporter and got Mr. Dorfman's phone number. I asked him if he would be interested in my poem. He requested that I fax it to him and did so immediately on September 18. Much to my surprise, not only did he like it, he wanted to know if I could come to Jennerstown, Pennsylvania to recite it at the ceremony. As a former journalist and broadcast TV news executive I have experienced many exciting moments in my professional career but that invitation was one I certainly bookmarked in my heart.

The event was only six days away. I quickly made plane reservations and alerted my family in Pittsburgh. On a beautiful Sunday morning on September 23 Mr. Dorfman displayed the huge symbol of America, one of the largest flags in the world. People came from miles around just to see it and touch it and to again feel good about themselves and their country.

The following day, remembrance day, it was cloudy and raining. I met Mr. Dorfman for the first time while he was directing members of the media on best camera angles. All of the local media were there on a vantage point on a hillside looking down on the Great American Flag. There she was 210 feet and 11 inches high and 411 feet wide. The stars were 13 feet in diameter and its stripes 16 feet tall. She was magnificent. We couldn't wait to touch it, to photograph it.

The pageantry was admirably small town America but big-time significance. The local high school band performed along with a local popular dance band. Speakers included a reverend, a local judge, his daughter, Mr. Dorfman and me. I will never forget when it was my turn to recite the poem. The wind and rain had intensified but no one left. No one moved and they were not about to. This event was historic and it was a tribute to those who lost their lives just 15 miles away in a rural field which was still a crime scene. Kinko's printing had contributed 4,000 copies of the poem to be passed out to the audience. While the crowd was estimated to be near three to four hundred the extra poems were passed out to schools and veterans organizations. The poem was warmly accepted and I found myself on the other side of a microphone being interviewed by the media. Several in the crowd laminated the poem and placed it at the actual crash site when it was later opened to the public. When the speakers had finished we all stood around the flag holding candles and singing as our tears blended with the rain.

Since September 24 the poem has generated a life of its own. It has been published in several newspapers, in magazines, read on radio and was featured on the front page of The National Flag Foundation's national quarterly magazine in the Fall of 2002.

I was requested to recite it at various meetings and events including my hometown of Lee's Summit, Missouri on the anniversary of 9/11 and at several Support Our Troops rallies and memorial services in 2003. It has been featured on the Internet by various web sites and readers have even made special links for the poem. Hopefully, it will someday be a song. For it is the story of renewed hope and a new found patriotism. It is the story of a former sunshine patriot. My friend stands first in line of 45 patriotic poems that proudly extol the many historic pages of this glorious country.

TABLE OF CONTENTS

I HELD THE FLAG TODAY

I held the flag today
It's been awhile, and it's not my style
But I touched it where it lay.
It's been in a drawer, it's been in a war
That took my dad away.
It brought back tears of grieving years
From that military day.
I remember the shoot - the gun salute
And I saw my mother pray.

I held the flag today
Mom nearly collapsed when they began the taps
For it took her breath away.
It was solemn and sad and she thought of my dad
Yet a smile broke through her dismay.
As they folded the banner in a reverent manner
My mom began to sway.
As they presented it to her - her mind was a blur
As she held the flag that day.

I held the flag today
Thinking of mom who is now gone,
Now I'm proud to say
I reclaim my land and pledge this hand
To honor and obey.
As my countrymen die ashamed am I
Before I could allay
All of the doubt I harbored throughout,
For I've been sympathy's prey.

I held the flag today
When the New York sky was terror most high
And our Capitol was in disarray.
Yet over a rural field heroes didn't yield

And caused their plane to stray.
As our eyes were locked as we gazed in shock
When the towers suddenly gave way.
Then those heroes in strife searching for life,
Their spirit had something to say.

I held the flag today
As our nation reached out to help pull them out,
For that's our American way.
To see our leaders react and vowed to attack
And that someone is going to pay.
I felt its fiber and thread, its living and dead
And I could hear it say
If we forget we'll always regret
Until our dying day.

I displayed the flag today
It's flying aloft that beautiful cloth,
Ready for the fray.
Whomever the foe, they'll reap what they sow
Starting from today.
I'm humble and proud and I say it aloud,
I'm an American-come what may.

Are you guys ready? Let's roll!

I WATCHED THEM GO

I watched with sorrow
I watched with woe
I bit my tongue
As I watched them go.

Yesterday they answered the role
Of various occupations
Now they're on a list
To join with other nations.

There they are, there am I
Anxieties build and mount,
Fearing to let go
Making every second count.

I am here to wish them well
I know nary a one
Yet I know all of them
Mother, father, daughter, son.

It wasn't long ago
With tears in our eyes
We stood on these docks
Gasping with sighs.

I held my husband's hand
I gazed into his heart
I felt our wedding vows
Until death do us part.

I pray the sorrows of tomorrow
May never surpass
The pains of the present
And the burdens of the their past.

And from the ship that call
The call to assemble
I know it all to well
As tender hearts tremble.

Every depth of sorrow
Lingers as they disband
Even the smallest infant
Senses a trembling hand.

Like leaves in deepest Autumn
Which reluctantly let go
To join their scattered brethren
On the grass and streets below.

No one moves as the vessel sails
On that sea of reality
Carrying that precious cargo
Into a storm of finality.

Where is history taking them?
Who among them will return?
What will we have garnered?
What will we have learned?

Those questions reverberate
From one generation to another
I lost my dearest husband
And I will love no other.

We, they, you bear a sacrifice
In our own patriotic way.
Yet saying good bye, perhaps forever
Are the saddest words we'll say.

I watched with sorrow
I watched with woe
I bit my lip
As I watched them go.

SHOCK AND AWE

I closed my eyes and looked away
When diplomacy failed
And sirens wailed
And anger ruled the day.
When loved ones held on
For soon they were gone
And we all began to pray.

While The Four Horsemen ride
Despite all of our failings
And all of our railings
We must put derision aside.
Whether we're pro or we're con
With our troops far beyond
Our unity must abide.

We sent over our best
To destroy that hand
That bloodied the land.
By a man possessed.
That manic regime
That death machine
That the willing came to arrest.

I flew my flag today
As the war we now dread
And the number of dead
Keeps mounting every day.
Some day this will end
Our world it will mend
And smiles will replace dismay.

Through the shock and the awe
Amid suspicion and doubt
We bantered about
There's one inescapable law.
Man is subject to error
On this planet so rare
It is he that is the flaw.

POW/MIA

They wore our country's colors
They swore freedom's vow
Now we have questions
Where? When? How?

Where are they?
Why don't they respond?
Why can't they answer?
Who holds their bond?

They were last seen
Defending Liberty's worth
We know they're out there
Somewhere on this earth.

Where do they repose?
Who dares to bind them?
How will we know?
How can we find them?

Our will will not fatigue,
We cannot be effaced
Every name is etched
They cannot be erased.

To those who test our will
With intent to defame
We never close a file,
We never forget a name.

Time may claim them
As time claims all.
Except our quest for closure
It's always on call.

Every name is precious
We owe each one a debt
History awaits them
And we shall never forget

See our flag of ebony
It beckons every day
With six haunting letters
POW-MIA

UNITED ON FLIGHT 93

Some read papers, some read books
Others engaged in talk
And unbeknownst to them
Four vipers watched the clock.

All were mostly strangers
Waiting for the call
To board a giant eagle
That on this day would fall.

They blended in with others
These snakes of foreign birth
Asps who came to crawl
On our freedom and our worth.

At Newark International
At Gate 17
They assembled and they boarded
The last day of a dream.

They didn't sit together
Nor did they communicate
But all their thoughts were one
To destroy and obliterate.

The manifest was small
Thirty-seven in number
And with a crew of seven
All would face the thunder.

The craft began to move
The time was eight o one
And forty minutes later
It was rising with the sun.

The land of San Francisco
Was six hours away
But those inside this fuselage
Would live their final day.

Out of the East toward the West
On this day to remember
Flew the 757
On the Eleventh of September.

Captain Dahl took command
With skill and concentration
They lifted off Runway 4
With a western destination.

Some could see the metropolis
Even those shining towers
Those canyons of steel
Like a basket full of flowers.

This chariot of wonder
Soared with peace and glee
But 40 minutes later
It lost tranquility.

This cabal of vipers
So many months ago
Planned this evil plot
Soon the world would know.

They sprang just like cobras
With heads adorned in red
They commandeered the plane
And the first hero now lay dead.

Fear and trepidation,
Confusion and alarm
Screams of desperation
All embraced by harm.

And passengers with phones
With fear in their eyes
Called throughout the land
That terror ruled the skies.

A stranger's voice commanded
From the intercom
This plane is now returning
On board there is a bomb.

The phones were like beacons
A refuge for their fear
They spoke of love and life
Of God, and to be near.

Passengers, Glick and Bingham
Beamer and Bradshaw
And so many others
Were telling what they saw.

Their phone mates on the other end
Were relaying information
About the towers, the Pentagon
And the devastation.

Suddenly Flight 93
Was turning toward the East
It ceased to be a plane
But a suicidal beast.

This missile on a course
For Washington D.C.
What their target was
Is still a mystery.

It now became apparent
To the passengers and crew
There was no escape
For all that would ensue.

Ninety-three was now united
They could not let this be
They made their final calls
Then stormed to victory.

These airborne heroes countervailed
With guts and dedication
They assailed the vipers nest
With surprise and consternation.

And from a field in Shanksville
In the state of Pennsylvania
They couldn't believe their eyes
A plane with signs of mania.

The missile was disarmed
It was hurling to the ground
Taking to their doom
All those honor bound.

These united fellow travelers
In less than an hour and a half
Became America's heroes
It became their epitaph.

Of sites and lives they did save
Someday it may unfold
But one thing is assured
Their story will be told.

That 40 men and women
Aboard Flight 93
They sent us all a message
They died for you and me.

THE VALIANT ONES

They came in great numbers
in their red chariots.
Many of these warriors of humanity,
laden with modern armament,
to combat flame, smoke and fear,
couldn't know that they would
soon be consumed
by the forces of hate, envy and evil.
As they looked skyward
as this monstrous foe,
this Goliath, this adversary,
they were in awe but not disarmed
for training and instincts
were autokinetic
and they began their fateful assent.
One laborious step at a time
one interminable flight at a time.
Soon they heard the pleas and screams,
this symphony from hell,
from a torrent of frightened humanity
rushing toward them,
racing to the safety below,
still, the valiant ones moved upward.
More of their brethren came rushing in
along with scores of comrades-in-arms
who swore to protect and defend.
They came with sirens pleading-
let us through, we're going in.
Medics and others joined that fray
all with a job to do.
And within the towers
the valiant ones,
weighed down with duty,
kept moving upward

15

Toward that conflagration.
of the unknown.
For this was a formidable foe
but somehow
they must find a way
to extinguish and preserve,
so they kept climbing higher.
They were fearless,
but fearful.
They were nervous,
but steady.
They were un daunting,
but vulnerable.
Undoubtedly
they thought of their families
and most of them must have prayed
as they neared Satan's door,
yet they kept moving upward.
These structures
were deeply wounded
growing weaker by
each precious second,
and the valiant ones knew it,
still they moved upward.
Then the first,
and soon the second,
halted their advance,
all of those within,
and all of those below,
they never had a chance.
A helpless nation watched it all
in disbelieving awe.
Then the tears they flowed
from fifty united states
followed by a tidal wave of prayer.
Then the word hero
was more than a name,

it wore many uniforms
on that bleak September day.
Worn by many creeds,
and many colors,
as many as the leaves of Fall.
Still, amid that flaming graveyard
pulling brick and steel,
were their remorseful comrades
fighting against the inevitable.
And the inevitable came.
Soon the loved ones
armed with photographs
and flowers, came looking for answers,
praying for miracles.
Grief and bewilderment
were etched on every countenance.
Our hearts cry out
for those heroes,
for those valiant ones,
who kept running in
who kept moving upward
gazing at hell
and heading for Heaven.

THE GREAT AMERICAN FLAG

I was made in Indiana sewn from special strands
Each fiber of my being came from loving hands.
I was formed to be a titan, the largest of them all
Yet equal in worth to large, medium or small.

Each star is thirteen feet without the slightest flaw
My stripes are even taller which gives me added awe.
And when I'm in full presence, in air or on the earth
Your eyes will gaze in wonder at my patriotic worth.

I was woven for a reason, all seasons, a cause
I require your approval. I need your applause.
I protect Colossus, Miss Liberty's tempest-tost
Lighting the way to freedom, ready at any cost.

I was not made to threaten, to belittle or to boast
I was created to empower, to be a friendly host.
I will try to raise your spirit when standing by my side
I will always be with. I will always abide.

Our stars have changed in number since 1782
But not our national colors - the red, the white and blue.
I am not the first to fly these hues nor will I be the last
We represent the future, the present and the past.

I'll do my part when called upon in the patriotic norm
On my historic journey I was there for Desert Storm
I even met, on a day so free, our hostages from Iran
When they honored Flight 93 I was near at hand.

Along with my brethren-we'll stand at our nations door.
We need your allegiance - in peacetime or in war,
To the Republic for which it stands,
To the future and all it demands.

And every time you touch me-go back to that day
When our freedom was in doubt and Mr. Key did say
And the rockets red glare, the bombs bursting in air
Gave proof through the night that our flag was still there.

I will rise when you need me. I am The Great American Flag

Jerry Plantz

WE STOOD IN THE RAIN

We stood in the rain on this historic day
Remembering September eleventh,
When infamy showed its evil hand
Akin to December seventh.

We stood on the hills overlooking a field
That cradled an object below,
Reaching out like Liberty's torch
This emblem was all a glow.

We stood in the mud and silently prayed
And we hardly made a sound.
Here in Pennsylvania,
Here in Jennerstown.

We stood as strangers, family and friends
To hear the words that day,
From a reverend, a poet and others
To help ease our dismay.

We stood in the wind stable and stoic
We came to lend our support,
To all who assembled this tapestry
This cloth we came to court.

We stood with our children, our mon's and our dads
Amid the American press,
Who sent to the nation their visuals and words
The object we came to caress.

We came down from the hills to that field below
To be near this national treasure,
To touch it, protect it and stand by it
It's a feeling you cannot measure.

As we stood in the rain, standing as one
Nurtured by this inspiration
No canvass or film could capture our hearts
We were indeed a conglomeration

As we stood in the rain around this square
Marveling at its makers,
It was wide, it was long, it was tall, it was strong
Spanning several acres.

As we stood in the rain on this dreary day
I know I shall always remember,
The year two thousand and one
The 24th day of September.

We stood with our tears, our candles and songs
Singing of liberty.
You could sense the spirit of American heroes
Nearby was Flight 93

As we left in the rain, the chill and the mist
Not once did our spirits lag,
We'll never forget, we touched and we saw
The Great American Flag.

REACHING OUT

There's seven red and six white
Flowing like a stream
Fifty stars adjoin the flight
Pleading to be seen.

The wind shares its glory
By helping it unfurl
It's a song, a poem, a story
It's a symphony of swirl.

The stars, the bars a field of blue
Beaming with every strand
Reaching out to all of you
This Republic for which we stand.

Of the wars and emancipation's
For which it was made
It has flown through generations
In an endless parade.

Yet all through its fame
As history rearranges
The colors stay the same
The message never changes.

Each section has a role
Meant to touch our hearts
For taken as a whole
We are the sum of all its parts.

It's been our inspiration
We're glad that we belong
To the world's greatest nation
And to sing our national song.

When it's sung you must not sit
To give its proper due
To all of those who died for it
That red, white and blue.

THE TALIBAN

How did you come to be?
Were you from the mold of Khan,
or the evil Reich of a thousand years
that never lasted a score?
How did you get to be the modern scourge,
the scourge of scourges hidden among a
nation of beautiful people?
You breathe new meaning into
the word convoluted.
You are the embodiment of a rudderless mind.
You are the distasteful bile of a regurgitated meal.
Even God, or Allah, hides in shame from your
barbaric intentions.
And the religion you proclaim is one you have defamed.
You have been rebuked by Muslim Mullahs of the world
Still you exist.
You have taken liberties with obvious interpretations
of the Quo' ran.
You strike fear instead of love.
You invoke hatred instead of compassion.
You harbor might instead of right.
You torture in place of healing.
You destroy temples of history.
You bring the unarmed to their knees.
You deny your women the basic rights of humanity.
And you cover them with veils of ignorance and subjugation.
You have taken a modern world full of wonders, beauty
and awe and reduced it to Cro-Magnon regression.
Your land is a land of war and you rule by the sword.
And now you spread your cancer throughout the globe.
And all in the name of Allah, an Allah you have caused to weep.
Indeed Allah is great-this you will soon see.

WE ONLY GET STRONGER

We've heard it all before,
those vitriolic words aimed at every generation.
They hurled it at doors and spit upon our flag.
They burned it and spurned it
but we only got stronger.

For all our foes in history since the War of 1812
we've been beyond their grasp like a giant with a swatter.
We repelled them like a gnat.
Their varied reasons are often an alchemy of
envy and disdain.
They always tried to harm us
and we only got stronger.

Even in our conflicts of the twentieth century
we always felt secure because we had the seas,
those walls of invincibility.
They gave us added protection
while the dreaded hand of harm
never touched our shores.
We were the ones who ventured out
to put an arm around a friend.
We transported our arms,
and our military might,
and our men and women.
to lift them off their knees,
and in doing so,
many of us never returned.
We're buried on their soil
and in our hour of grief
we only grew stronger.

We've even withstood - still today,
that verbal epithet - imperialism.
They failed to note we claimed no territory
after we raised our battered flags
on foreign soil.
Even when we reached out,
with aid to help their land,
they couldn't resist the insults
that we were ugly Americans
it is still prevalent today.
It confounds us
but we shrugged it off
as a harmless whim,
for we're use to it
and we only grew stronger.

Perhaps it was our hubris,
or was it wishful thinking,
that no one would dare
stand face to face
with the nation
with the mighty arm?
Who would dare to challenge a legend
a colossus, a dream
who lifts a lamp beside a golden door?
We thought - you could do it to others
but never to us.
If you did you'd surely regret.
But they did come
and they never looked us in the eye.
They came in disguise,
and in ugly surprise
they hit, and they ran,
and they hid.
It was a devastating blow
to our being and our psyche.
In their temporary triumphant glee

they didn't know
what we have always known,
that we will persevere
that we will plan their demise,
that it will only makes us stronger.

THE STORM OF 1991

You could see the clouds forming
In great discoloration
They were dire and ominous
Filled with trepidation.

The Middle East was churning
Creating yet another
A villain, a tyrant, a despot
Who took arms against his brother.

And now the dam had burst
This tidal wave Iraq
Flowing ever southward
In an unprovoked attack.

His armored troops were racing
They would not capitulate
To a small and harmless nation
Their neighbor called Kuwait.

It was over in a heartbeat
They took them to their knees
This despot of a man
Ignoring all their pleas.

He did not go unnoticed
He was warned to withdraw
For the world was looking in
Disapproving what it saw.

It didn't matter to this man
The one they call Hussein
He was beyond all reason
He was now a worldly bane.

He flexed his mighty arsenal
And challenged everyone
To come and take from him
His army and his gun.

But they did pick up the gauntlet
On land, sea and skies
They were the coalition
A rainbow of allies.

This storm in the desert
Of wind, swirl and gust
Was gaining momentum
Ready for a thrust.

And soon it would be blinding
Blotting out the sun
This storm of the century
In January - ninety-one.

This land of the Bible
This land of antiquity
Was again in the grasp
Of man's inequity.

The storm began to rain
For forty-three straight days
From a mighty armada
In devastating ways.

And when the order came
The storm engulfed the land
Sending men and tanks
Across this ancient sand.

There was no safe oasis
No shelter in this wake
For this despot of a man
Whose reign now did quake.

29

The sand was strewn with crimson
A monumental defeat
Still they scorched the land
In their ignominious retreat.

The storm was unrelenting
It swept with emancipation
With Bagdad in its path
It forecast vindication.

Then suddenly it expired
With an unexpected calm
The guns that fired no more
Gave way to salve and balm.

They had sent this despot home
Who came to despoil
This land of his brethren
With a war over oil.

His throne still exists
Watched by many nations
Yet he flaunts his disdain
Amid prevarications.

It's been more than half a score
Still he stands defiant
He still holds a sword
Waiting to be self-reliant.

But he knows there's an eagle
Soaring and circling above
Waiting for another gauntlet
Waiting to pick up the glove.

And should that day arrive
With a storm in the sun
Saddam can rest assured
It will be worst than Ninety-one.

VIETNAM

Vietnam - the scourge of four presidents
Eisenhower was the first
to hear this plea for help.
A few hundred advisors
swelled to 3 million troops
all in a span of a score
to face an indomitable foe
and their relentless devotion
to their cause.
If there was a vital reason,
if there was a noble cause,
it never fully resonated
on its citizenry.
Many vacillated between
arrow and laurel.
There were those
who found validation to continue
even while beleaguered.
The mighty levee of support,
reinforced over the years,
was now defective.
It's sinew was weakening,
there were no more sandbags,
it surrendered and gave way
pouring forth with a mighty surge
spreading over the countryside
engulfing everything in its path,
forcing political hands
to leave foreign lands
no hamlet, town or city
escaped divisiveness.
Slogan wars appeared
"America, Love It Or Leave It"
Were hurled against the doves.

They countered with equal vile
with many of their numbers
fleeing in exile to avoid conscription,
while those in uniform continued
to defend another slogan
"Keep communism out
of Southeast Asia,"
and dying by the score.
Abandoned and betrayed
by countryman
and leader alike,
their military might became effete
and their true potential and impact
were never unharnessed
as their full arsenal remained
half-empty.
Many Americans wanted to know why?
For what reason?
For whom?
Incompetence sat at the
diplomatic tables along with
impatience and naiveté.
In January of 1973
all enemies signed an accord
and the troops came home
and like Chamberlain,
who held a worthless piece of paper,
that accord soon was aflame
as if signed with invisible ink.
Then the lava from the North
flowed over the land
consuming city after city
until South Vietnam was no more.
The lava cooled
and crusted into a nation of red,
and the world went about its ways.
To those who fought to

prevent a calamity
the scars are deep,
yet we are a nation of many
and many did remember.
They grieved and cried
for that long list of dead
and erected a black ribbon of mourning
a wall of fifty six-thousand names,
a monument to those who
answered the call.
And to the veterans
who came home,
many washed your wounds
and took you in their embrace.
We, who number in that many,
will never forget
what you sacrificed.
Your duty to honor and country
will eventually be the balm
that erases from our memory
all of those facets that divided us.
But all of the facts,
and the consequences,
now belong to history,
and some of its pages
are untidy and regrettable,
still, many more are
replete with
love, honor, respect and
an undying gratitude and
a long belated greeting,
welcome home.

THE TWENTY-FIFTH OF JUNE

Why is there always someone
Who just won't be denied?
Who always flexes and bellows
And says that someone lied?

The ink was barely dry
On the Battleship Missouri
When it all rekindled again
The horror and the fury.

The year was 1950
Again the world was reeling
Not far removed from conflict
With wounds that still were healing.

The winds of war were horrific
On the 25th of June
When that far-off nation split in two
And now was facing doom.

Another foe, another threat
A challenge to our will
But we would only rest
When their goals were lying still.

Again we had to muster
The sinew of our young
Another generation
Summoned to fight as one.

Again we faced the terror
Bullets fired from Hell
We had to push them back
To the 38th Parallel.

We learned of Seoul and Pusan
And hills with lots of names
And human waves of lunacy
But we endured the flames.

Again they signed the papers
As we counted up our losses
And on this land we did defend
Now had stars and crosses.

Again - it had ended,
Like so many times before,
But this was called an action
Not an actual war.

They built a fence, a dividing line
Along this fiery border
And each is manned with sentries
To maintain peace and order.

Yet time came to steal from us
Our notoriety
We were slipping fast
Into obscurity.

We didn't ask for much
We didn't ask for more
Just a memorial
From this forgotten war.

It's not like this nation to forget
To deny glorification
So they went about the nations work
To appease our gratification.

And there it stands in Washington
A witness to a plea
To defend the South Koreans
To protect democracy.

It's made of granite
And men of stainless steel
A tribute to our generation
Who answered an appeal.

THE RISING SUN

The first bombs were verbal
In 1941
They were words of deception
From the Rising Sun.

These diplomats of cunning guile
Were careful what to say
While deep out in the ocean
Their fleet was underway.

This Emperor of Japan
With eyes on every Asian
Was courting our consent
While plotting his invasion.

An Yamamoto out at sea
Was coming from the West
With plane and ships of every size
On our national day of rest.

He paced with anxious moments
As he gazed upon his map
At a harbor we called Pearl
Was the center for his trap.

And then the moment came
To head into the wind
To lift this nest of wasps
And let the war begin.

They rose into formation
Against a rising sun
Ready to make history
Before this day was done.

On the Pacific jewel
This 7th day of December
It would become a cry
A day to remember.

This unsuspecting island
Rising from a sleep
Soon would suffer wounds
Fatal, dark and deep.

Some say we had the time
To stop them from afar
They found a harbor sub
And planes upon radar.

And all those stinging wasps
With unrelenting will
Were heading for a giant
Closing for the kill.

They caught a nation unaware
And acted with disdain
And soon a peaceful island
Was wounded and aflame.

And on the ground our planes did shine
Like stars in a constellation
And one by one they put them out
With total vitiation.

The second wave were bombers
Coming straight and low
Down to Ford Island,
Down to Battleship row.

They stood like sentries each a state
On this Sunday morning
And all their guns stood silent
There was never any warning.

They sunk the Arizona
It was an envious prize
It joined so many others
That were caught by surprise.

And everywhere a clarion call
To oust them from the skies
They answered back as best they could
Amid their pain and sighs.

With munitions spent and goal achieved
They destroyed an inert fleet
And left the scene boasting
Of a one-sided defeat.

The Pearl lay cracked and darkened
Amid a sky of flame
Amid a sea of carnage
With many names to blame.

When news reached the mainland
It destroyed their normalcy
And gripping them with fear
Was the hand of treachery.

Then the Colossus began to move
With manpower and resources
They got up off their wobbly knees
And started joining forces.

Four long years were spent
To disarm and dismember
A nation who sneak attacked
That Sunday in December.

While the Pearl is white and whole again
It is now historic soil
Where the Battleship Arizona
Is still leaking oil.

That rising sun that scorched us
It left a legacy
A war, a cause, a motto
That day of infamy.

NORMANDY AND NOT CALAIS

As far as the eye can see my friend
As far as the eye can see
How in the world can we defend
What is facing us at sea?

As far as the eye can see my friend
There are ships of every size
Destroyers and Transports end to end
Coming to seize this prize.

As far as the eye can see my friend
And now we hear the din
Of bursting salvos that will rend
Our walls and will to win.

As far as the eye can see my friend
And now they're loading men
Along with guns and tanks they'll send
And now they're coming in.

As far as the eye can see my friend
Amid our repulsive roar
This is a breach we cannot mend
And now they're coming ashore.

As far as the eye can see my friend
They come without a quay
Is this the beginning of the end?
Was all this meant to be?

As far as the eye can see my friend
It's Normandy not Calais
We misread our enemy's trend
It's not the other way.

As far as the eye can see my friend
This will be the longest day
History will know if we can defend
This Normandy and not Calais.

Jerry Plantz

WINGS OF TUSKEGEE

They had the blood of their ancestors
With valor as well
They had wings of silver
That could fly into hell.

Everyone a volunteer
Everyone was black
They all had a mission
To fly and to attack.

The first historic class
Trained in 1941
At Tuskegee, Alabama
Under a segregated sun.

Despite the separate air
And the color of their skin
They trained with a quest
That burned deep within.

From the long gray line
Came a stern black knight
Benjamin O Davis Junior
Ready to lead, ready to fight.

This bright star in the cosmos
Among the first with wings
His was just the beginning
Of monumental things.

The eaglets swelled in number
With Davis above the norm
A career that ended proudly
With a four star uniform.

Like generations before them
Subject to doubt, subject to test
They silenced all the doubters
When ranked among the very best.

They emblazoned the ninety-ninth
The three hundred and thirty-second
With sacrifice and courage
Whenever freedom did beckon.

And history will attest
These squadrons of flight
Also shattered myths
Some black, some white.

They held the steady reins
Of their noble generation
A war within a war
Military segregation.

Despite the indignation
Their quest would not be fallow
Their final page was written
With the historic pen of hallow.

Then the word United
In nineteen-forty-eight
Suddenly had meaning
It could not alienate.

At last - vindication
Order ninety-nine eighty-one
America's Armed Forces
United now as one.

Those airmen forged a legend
With heroic combat deeds
Those wings of Tuskegee
Squadrons of steeds.

They're etched on scrolls
Among the Fifty-fourth
Among the Buffalo soldiers
And others who came forth.

Oh modern aviators
When in the sky you wander
Hold them in your hearts
Who shared that wild blue yonder.

Your brothers led the way
Those black heroes of the sky
The pride of Tuskegee
Who proved they could fight and fly.

THE SAVING GENERATION

My being cries out to reflect on a special generation of Americans.
If I could present a plaque, a soliloquy, or a tribute it would speak of a generation of Americans whose lasting renown has long been awaited.
It is a generation of citizens who were suddenly, and unexpectedly, thrust into the maelstrom of peril and fright.
Like others before them, they were unceremoniously called to defend and mend the nation on their watch. And like their founding fathers they unselfishly stepped forward and carried the spirit of freedom in their hearts with delicate humility.
They rallied to repel and defeat the specter of tyranny both on the home-front and over there.
With concerned haste and determination they answered the call. The call for an indomitable spirit and an unwavering faith that democracy and this republic would prevail.
They were not the gallant patriotic men and women in military uniforms,
yet they served with equal valor and devotion.
These were the fighting civilians of the two score generation.
Armed with riveting guns, machinery and determination they went to work.
They rolled up their sleeves in the factories and mills.
They rolled up their sleeves on the farms and in the cities.
They rolled up their sleeves with sacrifice, war bonds, ration stamps and songs.
They rolled up their sleeves because their generation, like many before them, was summoned to fight yet another war, and this one not far removed from the one to end all wars.
They did not drive the tanks-they made them.
They did not fly the planes-they made them.
They did not sail the ships-they made them.
They did not fire the weapons - they made them.
They did not wear the military uniforms-they made them.

47

They found Miss Liberty bleeding so they cradled her body and healed her.

The efforts of their toils, along with their military brethren, stopped the unchecked tyrants.

With their allies they silenced the guns, calmed the waters, stopped the bloodshed and sealed the epicenter of turmoil and hate.

And when the drums had ceased and tranquillity returned they again blended in with the great fabric of America.

They sought no special laurels, no parades and no monuments for their perpetual achievements.

With subdued humility and pride they reminded us that the torch had not gone out on their watch.

America was in danger and they responded.

It is to their indelible memory and their patriotic devotion that we dedicate these words so that all generations, especially the youth, will forever remember their brief moment in history and time - a heartbeat of a millennium- and that they were the binding human threads that comprise this tapestry of democracy we call America-they were a saving generation - the civilian generation of World War Two.

STARS IN MY WINDOW

It was a sad burden a task death always assigns.
To sort ones personal treasures
and have the courage to see it through.
Grandparents are special.
Their memories, like their keepsakes,
should be jewels for kin to share.
And when life moves on it's an onus we must bear,
to sort, disperse or destroy.
Box after box,
chest after chest,
trunk after trunk of
clothes, trinkets, jewelry,
photographs and souvenirs.
In my labor of remorse I came upon a chest
labeled World War Two.
I opened it with care and neatly packed inside
were things I never knew.
Ration stamps and books
and magazines with stories of the war.
Patriotic posters of female riveters
and Uncle Sam pointing to me.
An ominous warning that
"loose lips sink ships."
There was a newspaper account of
the five Sullivan brothers
who all died aboard
the same ship
torpedoed by the Japanese.
There within a frame of glass
a large photograph new to all,
of my uncles Jim and Ray.
Dressed in Army brown
with their lone PFC stripe.
with arms around each other

smiling proudly for their mom.
These were my Army uncles
that the war would deprive me of.
I started to cry.
Why? I'll never know.
Then mom knelt beside me
with an understanding smile.
Her handsome brothers
she remembered well
even though she was just a child.
She reached inside the chest,
as if she had been here before,
to a cigar box.
that contained a small white banner,
a very special banner, trimmed in red.
In the center were two fading stars of gold.
One for uncle Jim,
the other for uncle Ray.
Then, as if to summon me,
a faded yellow paper fell upon my lap.
It was an official telegram
with dreaded woeful words,
words that raced across my eyes.
"We regret to inform you that your sons
Army Private First Class Raymond"…
Oh no!
"and Army Private First Class James"…
Oh, no!
"died while defending their country"…
Oh my heroic uncles!
The missive drummed on
"on behalf of a grateful nation"…
I could not finish
as I felt the heavy hearts
of my grandparents and I
tried to fathom how they withstood
the dreaded consequences

of this faceless messenger,
a communiqué of death that made its
way to thousands of
mothers, fathers and loved ones
in a nation fighting a world war.
My mom, her eyes glistening
and fighting back memories of
when her parents read that message,
handed me the service flag
and said.
Keep this special treasure
it represents part of our
family, our heritage, our country.
My hands were trembling
as we embraced
each touching the service flag.
I kissed the two stars and
I told her that never again
will this visual epitaph
be cached or hidden.
in the embrace of a chest of memories.
It now is on display
within our humble home.
Because of it, because of them,
there's a replica
in the center of my bay window.
A service flag with stars.
Two stars of blue signifying life
the lives of our son and daughter,
who now wear uniforms,
who proudly serve their country
on distant foreign shores.
And there on the mantle
amid our family photographs,
along with their great grandparents,
along with their great uncles,
in the uniforms of their country.

51

they proudly sit smiling back at me.
Now every night while on my knees
I pray for all our service men and women
and to their loved ones
who pine, pray and ponder.
I want the world to know
I have stars in my window.

EXECUTIVE ORDER NO. 9066

The Japanese Empire had struck.
It came without warning or compassion.
The fires were barely extinguished at the massacre of a Hawaiian harbor
known as Pearl when a blanket was placed over the U.S. Constitution and ignored
and shuttered for more than a hundred thousand Americans.
Fellow citizens, fellow patriots.
A nervous nation, satiated with ignorance and intolerance, spurred on by suspicion and fear,
began to threaten the very lives of fellow Americans because they were of Japanese descent.
It permeated even the Nation's Capitol when on February 19, 1942 the president signed his name
to Executive Order No. 9066.
With it went the legal rights of all Americans of Japanese ancestry.
Gone was the writ of habeas corpus and due process of law and the most embarrassing insult of all, the creation of relocation centers.
Japanese-Americans were uprooted from their homes and escorted to 10 detention centers.
Americans who once lived and toiled in neighborhoods, where they were taught in American classrooms, and they lived the American dream.
Were once was employment and livelihood-there was now food lines and idleness.
Were once there were picket fences-there was now barbed wire.
Were once there was unbridled freedom-they were assembled behind closed metal doors.
It wasn't he harshness of their existence that flogged at their endurement It was the indignity
of sweeping generalities and national distrust that pained them the most.
Many lived in overcrowded spaces.
They all were imprisoned with a blanket indictment of subversion

Many of whom didn't know what the word meant let alone carry out its definition.
Those who did pass the rigid test of allegiance served in special military units to fight against
the land of their ancestors, the Land of the Rising Sun.
Those who did muster this indignation acquitted themselves with distinction-they did so as Americans. Japanese Americans.
When the insanity of the world ended they returned to whatever life could offer.
Their psychological anguish was paramount.
Their health in stages of various complications and their hearts as Americans broken.
Finally the words "We're sorry" echoed from the halls of justice as reparations and redress were in order.
Some recompense aided some, but for others, no amount of money could wash away the stigma of distrust, unwantedness and racism.
Succeeding generations of Japanese-Americans would know of the plight of their ancestors.
That their president and country turned their back on them and sent them into exile. Executive order number 9066 will be passed down to future generations so that they may know It did happen here.
It happened to us.
It could happen to you.
It could happen to anyone.
It must not happen again.

THERE'S A MEMORIAL IN KANSAS CITY

*Recited at the rededication ceremonies of the World War I Liberty
Memorial in Kansas City, Mo. on May 25, 2002.*

There's a memorial in Kansas City
And they named it Liberty
Our grandfather took us there
When he was eighty-three.

We found this noble treasure
When I was just a lad
It tells about a war
A war that claimed his dad.

It's nestled on a hill
With a panoramic view
Of a city with a heart
And a welcome mat for you.

On that dedication day
They came from foreign lands
To this international tribute
Carved from loving hands.

It's a tapestry of history
With a tower in the center
Like a beacon in a harbor
Protecting all who enter.

There are four imposing sentries
Peering from the tower
With hands at rest and ready
On swords of righteous power.

Patriotism, honor, courage, sacrifice
Are carved upon these four
They duly represent
All who fought this war.

And facing them with covered eyes
As if to hide their shame
Are Future and Memory
With messages of blame.

These two warning Sphinxes
From ancient history
Have given us notice
That war breeds misery.

And in those museums
Replete with artifacts
Are names of many heroes
Who died in the attacks.

There in woeful numbers
There in Memory Hall
Among his fallen peers
Was our name upon that wall.

Far off in that foreign soil
Their sprits were inhumed
Yet here in Kansas City
Their legacy's entombed.

Over there In Flanders Field
From Belgium to Verdun
Lies this generation
Who fought in World War One.

There's always those who pay the price
Before the guns do cease
Whomever they are, wherever they are
May their souls rest in peace.

And the loved ones of the fallen
Proudly did display
A simple Star of Gold
It had so much to say.

To those that came in numbers
To this site so long ago
It's written in our hearts
Of their anguish and their woe.

Yet imbued within us
Is their eternal legacy
There's hope, and love and life
In preserving liberty.

It echoes all around this site
Echoes with every step
Freedom and Democracy
And Lest We Forget.

And when this spirit on the hill
Was old, and weak and trembling
This city knelt beside it
And soon began assembling.

For modern day America
Rallied to their call
Even the children
Pitched in to save it all.

They restored this sacred symbol
With a strong abiding will
To make it last forever
This marvel on the hill.

Our granddad brought us here
Not for praise, pride or pity
He wanted us to know
There's a memorial in Kansas City.

A SUMMER OF SHAME

If you look at the flag close enough
Amid the stars and the hue
You'll discover a tear of shame
From 1932.

They were called the Bonus Army
This Army of duress
They appeared in massive numbers
With symptoms of stress.

It wasn't long ago
They had rifles in their hands
Defending this nation's freedom
And fighting in foreign lands

Now they advanced on Washington
On to Capitol Hill
To show they were united
For a controversial bill.

They came from the farms
The docks and the mines
The shops and mills
And assembly lines.

The country was inert
Caught in a deep depression
Caught in a free-fall
Caught in a steep recession.

These veterans needed help
Just to stay alive
They needed it now
If they were to survive.

Single men and families
Walking side by side
Losing all they had
The last of which was pride.

Nearly twenty thousand strong
Who came from everywhere
These, the jobless veterans
Who once went over there.

They were a scar on the land
They slept wherever they could
Under cloth, straw and mud
Under paper, tin and wood.

Order had prevailed
As May turned to June
And then came the vote
That would seal their doom.

There was a wisp of hope
When the House it voted yea
But the die was cast
When the Senate voted nay.

The budget had been exhausted
These men would get no more
These men would have to wait
These men who fought the war.

Dejected and despondent
Most began to leave
Some want on aimlessly
Others home to grieve.

But this was not the final scene
As thousands stayed the course
Penniless and homeless
They'd have to leave by force.

An anger turned to rage
As tempers began to flare
In the summer of 32
Shame embraced the air.

The desperate and the forlorn
Bonded with one another
While the Army drew their sabers
Ready to strike their brother.

Words and fists began to flail
As reason was put on hold
And our darkest day in history
Was ready to unfold.

And General Douglas MacArthur
Who was in command that day
Heard the call from Hoover
Clear them without delay.

And soon the pride of West Point
With Patton and Eisenhower
Were moving at a gallop
Showing all their power.

As the advancing US Army
Met them face-to-face
Most in tears carried out
This order of disgrace.

While no one fired a shot that day
American blood was shed
Hundreds had been injured
And an innocent child lay dead.

And soon that shanty town
That the armed came to raze
On July 28th
Was suddenly ablaze.

And beautiful Lady Liberty
In a harbor miles away
Was shedding a tear
And her torch began to sway.

And nearby in Arlington
Where our military lay
Was heard the sound of sobbing
Beneath the ground that day.

MacArthur ruled the hour
He had freed an ugly clot
To him 'twas a revolution
To him a communist plot.

History has shown
That upheaval was never real
That deception never arrived
Nor treason behind the wheel.

They epitomized the poem
Of the homeless, tempest-tost
These the wretched refuse
The poor, the needy, the lost.

Time is the ultimate healer
It's a soothing mystery
It cannot alter the past
Or change our history.

When the army of the present
Met the army of the past
Both borne of a country
With the same mold and cast.

When the grass was green again
With a clear reflecting pool
And the country rose from gloom
To rekindle and retool,

They felt the pain and stigma
Of a summer like no other
When two armies clashed
Brother against brother.

It's not within our nature
To record just our glory
We acknowledge imperfections
Of our never-ending story.

And one of those was written
About the vets who fought a war
Who wanted what was promised
Nothing less, nothing more.

We regret and we remember
And we vowed to always rue
To never relive the shame
Like the summer of thirty-two.

THE DOCTRINE

Many factions wanted to know
What was all this about?
Why did we strike a blow
To throw the Spanish out?

Was it the Doctrine
That warned and made it clear
That we were locked in
To protect our hemisphere?

Or was it the Maine
And those Jingoists
Who became a bane
With sabers and fists?

Whatever the cause or core
We exhausted all debate
Then declared war
In 1898.

From Cuba to Manila
With arms to permeate
With cavalry and flotilla
We were there to palliate

In less than a year
We stopped annexation
No more would we fear
A foreign occupation.

It's in this hemisphere
All nations do know
This doctrine we revere
From President Monroe.

THE BUFFALO SOLDIERS

Eighty years of hoof beats
Eighty years of strife
Eighty years of honor
Eighty years of life.

Four scores of riding
Gleaning fame upon a horse
Buffalo soldiers
Gleaning fame amid remorse.

History first records them
In post civil war
In forts or at a gallop
Guarding our western door.

The 9th and 10th were ready
This cavalry dressed in blue
Began their western march
Where trouble would ensue.

The Indians of the West
With war paint on their face
Gazed in consternation
These men of another race.

These were not white men
Their skin was like the night
They had horses, food and rifles
An enemy who could fight.

Their deeds were recorded
Throughout the Indian land.
Sitting Bull, Geronimo
Comanches, Cheyenne.

The red man had knighted them
And their legend did grow
These averring horsemen
Like the rugged buffalo.

These were the elite
On horseback in the West
The pride of their race
A black cavalry at its best.

Still, like their predecessors
Who were always shunted
They too relived the words
Black, last, unwanted.

From Mexico to Kansas
They responded for the nation
Protecting all its assets
With proud validation.

They guarded communications
Telegraph, stage and mail.
They even mapped the land
Land they could not avail.

Rustlers, bandits, gunmen,
Thieves in the night
They had to face them all
With ridicule and spite.

They kept on riding tall
Generation after generation
San Juan Hill to the Rio Grande
Fighting for an expanding nation.

Change is always inevitable
And often not amendable
After World War Two
Their units were expendable.

But not their glorious legacy
It's replete among our pages
Part of America's story
Passed down through the ages.

They were the 9th and 10th
Of a special cavalry
These the Buffalo Soldiers
Free sons of slavery.

SEPARATE BUT UNITED

My coat is blue and his of gray
Colors of a different perspective
Each chose a separate way
Through a conscientious directive.

Blessed was the day when he was born
Where came the seed of dissension?
Why he responded to a rebel horn
Is beyond my comprehension.

He took up arms and so did I
Each to defend a conviction
Parting company with a mutual sigh
And fearful predilection.

How could a father and a son
Each with a fanatic devotion,
To take up powder and gun
And place their cause in motion?

We parted bravely amid our tears
With faith, gun and rod
Soon the months turned into years
Wondering where was God.

There upon a span, a ridge
With orders to defend
There upon a vital bridge
My world came to an end.

There at war's door
Weighing victory or defeat
Amid the canon's roar
A boy fell at my feet

A thousand spears had pierced my heart
As he gazed into my eyes
And all those days that kept us apart
Merged with deadly surprise

No wall impedes this embrace
I feel his youthful days
His play, his faith, his smiling face
And all his innocent ways.

The coming moments are the ones I dread
He's sinless and need not atone
Heal his wound, take me instead
Please don't call him home.

He doesn't merit this fearsome fate
His life is ebbing away.
Oh son! Please wait, wait, wait
Oh how can I stop this day?

And how does one undo regrets
And to exist in a world of if?
That beats, beats like castanets
Reminding me of our rife.

Dear lad and soldier your fight is done
So noble, brave and pristine
Take him Lord, my precious son
From this grave so bloody obscene

The Union or separate states?
Does it justify
Years of heated debates
And the dead to rectify?

I lost a son, he lost a cause
It's something I can't comprehend
Who will run, who will pause?
Will we start all over again?

My soul is effete and my body is numb
And the question throbs in my brain
When it's over and we total the sum
Will mankind ever be sane?

FORWARD FIFTY-FOURTH

The Emancipation Proclamation
In 1863
Now accepted Negroes
At forts and ships at sea

They were black, proud and free
These men of the Fifty-fourth
This military unit
Assembled in the North.

They were second among their race
To serve in the infantry
They earned every stripe
They were black, proud and free.

The Massachusetts Fifty-fourth
All enlisted men
Six hundred and fifty
Not an officer within.

Only whites held the rank
For directing men of color
One was Colonel Shaw
With men from a nation's cellar.

Thirteen dollars a month
Was unjust compensation
The whites were offered more
Because of pigmentation.

Distrust and low esteem
Gnawed at their dignity
Yet nothing could dissuade them
To fight for liberty.

71

They first became as one
In the winter of sixty-three
With uniforms of blue
For all the South to see.

Bullets and shells were the least
To test their bravery
They knew if they were caught
They'd know of slavery.

They had a noble mission
Which all of them behooved
To fight with pride and honor
And this they'd have to prove.

History was waiting with pen in hand
When they marched into the war
At a fort on Morris Island
Off the South Carolina shore.

Destiny awaited them
On the 18th of July
The Fifty-fourth was ready
Ready with banners high.

Fort Wagner was a challenge
If to attack by land
The sea and swamp were on its sides
And in the front was sand.

The day began with canon fire
It was their first resort
It continued on throughout the day
To weaken that mighty fort.

Then General Quincy Gilmore
Gave that fatal command
Mount a frontal assault
With the Fifty-four at hand.

Colonel Shaw drew his saber
Near the fort by the sea
This regiment was ready
They were black, proud and free.

Never was their more evidence
Of a baptism of fire
The Fifty-fourth began to move
With fear and desire.

This day they were a vanguard
Of an army and a nation
They would lead the charge
With prestige or degradation.

The pace began to quicken
As the day was losing light
And now the world would see
If the blacks knew how to fight.

With fixed bayonets
The assault was underway
The start of their finest hour
The end of doubt and dismay.

Into the greatest storm
From which there was no protection
Bombs and bullets from everywhere
Like centuries of rejection.

73

Yet onward the six hundred
Just like the Light Brigade
Into the jaws of death
Into the history they made.

Hero after hero
Toward the enemy at hand
Past their fallen comrades
Who lay dead upon the sand.

The Confederates fired in awe
At a never-ending wave
Of the fighting Fifty-fourth
With their Union to save.

They had reached the outer walls
Of this well defended site
Their numbers were fewer
They would not last the night

There at the top of a parapet
Colonel Shaw amid the strife
Shouting Forward, Fifty-fourth
The young hero lost his life.

Sergeant William H. Carney
Wounded and still with mettle
Planted the colors at the wall
And received the highest medal.

The blue was overwhelmed
By the Confederates of gray
They slowly crawled to safety
Passed those who fell that day.

When the day was over
In this battle by the sea
Now more than ever
They were black, proud and free.

The Union whites embraced them
With a rousing ovation
Could there ever be any doubt
Of their devotion to a nation.

The battle lasted 60 days when
The Island was finally taken
And the Union flag was hoisted
Where once it was forsaken.

There are those who question still
Where the fighting had thundered
Like those of the Light Brigade
Someone had blundered.

Yet none would ever doubt
Of their courage by the sea
Of the famous Fifty-fourth
Who were black, proud and free.

Jerry Plantz

TWO HUNDRED AND SEVENTY-TWO WORDS

Four months removed from the summer heat
On this sacred Union soil
Where the southern general sounded retreat
And had his troops uncoil.

Here is where they drew the line
Those coats of blue and gray
Now they lie in graves of time
Where their souls no longer stay.

Now men of words, wealth and station
Came to dissertate
Yet the man who led the nation
Came to consecrate.

Amid those words that he read
Two hundred and seventy-two
He praised the Union and the dead
With thoughts that did imbue.

His soothing words each a balm
Was meant to ease the pain
It sounded like a Sunday psalm
They shall not have died in vain.

With more than power to add or detract
His words reverberated
As he eulogized this famous tract
Of souls emancipated.

This government of the people
A nation full of worth
By the people, for the people
Shall not perish from the earth.

The Union that he pledged to save
And that final resting place
Along with the speech he gave
Ennobled the Human Race.

An encomium of candor
Terse, solemn and euphonious
This speech of rapport
Was sanguine and harmonious

I remember every word he said
It moves my entity
That eulogy that he read
In 1863.

When your spirit needs a lift
Or words from heaven sent
Then seek out this gift
From our 16th President.

Those words of dedication
From his world of duress
Those words of inspiration
From The Gettysburg Address.

ACT THREE, SCENE TWO-LINCOLN'S ASSASSINATION

Act three, scene two
On this historic Christian day
Of a man on a cross
Who died to lead the way.

Act three, scene two
Laughter filled the night
But a powder keg of doom
Was ready to ignite.

Act three, scene two
The finale of a man
An incomplete play
An evil treacherous hand.

Act three, scene two
A play to make one laugh
Not tonight, not ever more
For a country torn in half.

Act three, scene two
Was the last view with his wife
As he smiled upon an actor
While another took his life.

Act three, scene two
In 1865
From a Derringer 44
From a cause barely alive.

Act three, scene two
The villain took the stage
Spewing forth his deed
Then fled in fit of rage.

Act three, scene two
The specter of death drew near
To claim a president
That history would endear.

Act three, scene two
The finale of a man
The beginning of a legend
The Union still does stand.

THAT OUR FLAG WAS STILL THERE

Like an unrelenting flood
America was rearranging
With expansion in their blood
Ever spreading, ever changing.

Hubris and profit
Were claiming Indian lands
Thus Tecumseh and Prophet
Took matters in their hands.

When their effort was denied
They moved their warriors North
And there they were allied
With the British boiling forth.

Then there were the Hawks
With a war to incite
Undoing the locks
That kept them from flight.

A grievance list they made
An assessment of free men
Frontier, land and trade
To impressment of seaman.

In 1812 in that mid year
They voted to take up arms
Their call was like the chanticleer
Alerting cities and farms.

Thirty years had passed
Since peace was anew
Again the die was cast
A war of dejavu.

With canons and guns
With rights to amend
Went fathers and sons
With a land to defend.

On a ship or in a garrison
Historians now had names
Like Perry, Jackson, Harrison
And Washington in flames.

The turmoil stretched the rack
Of a strong abiding force
However, some did lack
The will to stay the course.

At a Hartford convention
The Union began to bleed
They had a secret intention
To cease and secede.

Not the city of Baltimore
At a patriotic fort
They faced the guns of war
With military deport.

Here's the enemy to defeat
Everything they saw
This massive British fleet
Ready for the coup de grace.

Beneath the stars and bars
Somehow they must prevail
With the shield of Mars
Then canons began to wail.

On that historic morn
The 13th of September
Came a turbulent storm
Meant to maim and dismember.

Thrust and parry
Pain and dismay
Loud and scary
Throughout the day.

The night was illuminated
Trapped in a fiery flight
Until it was liberated
By the dawns early light.

There on the sea
Beyond the death and the din
Was Francis Scott Key
Watching the bravest of men.

Through a telescope
His eyes began spying
For that banner of hope
Was it still flying?

And there it stood
Waving for all to see
With its cloth and its wood
Waving to him at sea.

Key's words began to flow
In true rapid manner
The world would soon know
Of The Star - Spangled Banner.

The enemy from the realm
Had given up the quest
On mount or at the helm
No victory would they wrest.

Peace treaties were signed
After thirty months of strife
Canada remained defined
Yet growth returned to life.

Some still opine today
What a senseless confrontation
While others will say
We had to defend the nation.

But all were assured
That Americans were aware
The Union had endured
That our flag was still there.

FROM A QUARREL TO A REVOLUTION

The volley's were fired
Long before Lexington green
Their salvos came as unjust laws
Fired to destroy a dream.

The motherland was but an isle
A land we could not relate
King George gave us laws
That wasn't open to debate.

Pioneers starting over
In a land so fresh and new
And we didn't need royalty
To tell us what to do.

The British failed to acknowledge
Or at least to comprehend
That we had nothing in common
And their hold on us would end.

We were ruled by a hand
That we couldn't even see
We had no representation
We just had tyranny.

Whether by accident
Or whether by plan
Outside a Boston Custom House
Five died by their hand.

We had independent thoughts
With unified greetings
And all this was expressed
At many town meetings.

Boston's Old South Meeting House
Was our anvil and our steel
That helped to free a nation
And melt the royal seal.

They burdened us with levies
Even on our tea
We had to send a message
So we threw it in the sea.

It stirred and moved the crown
These brash colonies
They sent a great militia
To bring us to our knees.

We had patriots like Adams
Otis and Livingston,
Henry and Franklin
And Thomas Jefferson.

They were joined by many others
With resolve and intent
To ignore the rules and laws
Made without consent.

They listed with pen and paper
What our nation laments
It simply began
When in the course of human events.

And what was once a quarrel
Became a revolution
And a man named Washington
Was to bring us restitution.

And this infant of a nation
With a cast of minutemen
Struggled to survive
In a war we had to win.

Often outnumbered
And even without food
They had a surfeit full of purpose
That nurtured every mood.

And with the aid of France
The war came to an end
Eight laborious years
That began with power and pen.

There is so much to chronicle
About this generation
About our founding fathers
Who breathed life into a nation.

FIFTY-SIX PATRIOTS

Ink flowing on paper
Forming words of frustration
Tyranny had created
A defiant declaration.

The course of human events
Impelled them to separation
Recording every injustice
And every indignation.

Sent to an insensitive king
For his dastardly deeds
With an arrogant ruling hand
Ignoring all their needs.

It was a stirring document
A parchment, a proclamation
Declaring all men equal
Declaring a free nation.

Fifty-six names
Colonists no more
Citizens of states
Americans to the core.

Fifty-six traitors
The crown claimed them to be
Rebuking their insurrection
On land and on the sea.

This birth of revolution
Where patriotism thrives
They were sacrificing fortunes
And fighting for their lives.

Their pledge was resolute
This paper that excites
Endowed by their Creator
With unalienable rights.

The parchment still endures
A haven for whom it relates
That these Colonies shall remain
Free independent states.

Fifty-six patriots
Braving their transcendence
Signed that precious paper
The Declaration of Independence.

THEY WORE CROSSES OF RED

They do wear helmets and uniforms
and go in with the initial wave.
They fire no weapons and bear no arms
yet their presence is just as perilous.
They are pervious to bullets and fear
and they are ever aware of their presence.
But their eyes and their ears
have more pressing needs
as they scan in front and behind,
waiting for the call,
waiting for that name
that triggers a plea for haste
to come to the aid
with their pills and their balm
to embrace a fallen comrade.
They must summon the will
the nerve and the skill
to defeat the pain
of these frail and damaged bodies.
Their bag of panacea must contain
healing and soothing words
to those with a fearful mind,
and too many times
they are the last face they see,
the last voice they hear,
as their soul is freed to rest.
They have little time for sorrow,
not even time for prayer,
for if they did it would
consume their souls,
for they call out your name
again, again and again.
Corpsman, medic, nurse,
without hesitation they go

wherever the cross is needed.
And when it's over,
when the wounded are safely at home
and are part of a healing world,
they'll reflect and recall
with grateful admiration
those comrades who fought beside them
whose weapons were crosses of red.

THE FLAG BEARERS

He's brave, tough, has a motive to kill
His courage never does lag.
What is it he places on top of the hill?
Why it's just the American flag.

Then falls to his knees beneath the banner
As crimson covers his shirt
A word with his God in a pleading manner
Then his body becomes inert.

To him this mission was much ado
As the flag begins its swaying
And no one moves above the hue
For the frightened they are praying.

Except for one who beholds the sight
And he begins to rationalize
Why must we always kill and fight?
As tears flow from his eyes.

My brother died on this very hill
And am I here to do the same?
If only I could summon the will
And who is really to blame?

Eat with our hands and wash from a pot
And the dirt to account for our bed.
Gambling with death with each single shot
And here to avenge our dead.

Then his conscience begins to veer
As he sees the wavering flag.
His mounting courage begins to sear
I'll not wear a cowards tag.

91

Explosions abound with shrapnel and fears
As his buddies fall by his side
Go get that flag we see no tears
And show America's pride.

The staff is falling your decision is quick
And your tears they mix with blood
You now feel the meaning of the cloth and the stick
As you plunge the staff into the mud.

The wind unfurls it with a thrust
As it waves and calls to all
Hear me don't dishonor that trust
Of those who had to fall.

The bearer is smiling on top of that hill
He knows they have taken the crest
He also knows that soon he'll be still
As the pain swells deep in his chest.

Three enemy soldiers challenge your raid
And are denied what you possess
From a crossfire of buddies who come to your aid
For the flag is still in your caress.

You fall to your knees, tears in your eyes.
And blood trickling down from your head
A word with your Lord, a last desperate cry
Then add to the column of dead.

The enemy disperses in full retreat
And the hill is a sea of GI's.
Sometimes a victory isn't a treat
Not when your best buddy dies.

The fighting has silenced the mighty guns
And now to collect that tag
Of the brothers, the fathers, the uncles, the sons
Who fell while defending the flag.

I had to come back to this very hill
To the bravery that spurred us on
To the bearers who summoned the will
To lead us above and beyond.

The graves abound solemn and cold
And a church bell echoes its tolls
And there standing like a titan of old
Is our flag waving over the their souls.

I remember them all who died on this soil
Their symbols are adorned in white.
With crosses like Chavez, Walker, and Doyle
And stars like Horwitz and Hite.

Of Jackson, Shultz, Ravi and Smart
O'Hara, Lipinski and Mann
All indelible etched in my heart
Now buried beneath this land.

What obsesses most - this no name hill
And the men who lived its story
It's not the ground -it's the men if you will
The GI's - who saved Old Glory.

Jerry Plantz

WE DO SALUTE

We do salute
From the daughters of the Revolution
To the spirit of the minutemen
To those who died for all
And to those who did defend.

We do salute
All of those who guard our shores
We hold in deepest regard
The men and women in uniform
Of the U. S. Coast Guard.

We do salute
Those that go into the wild blue yonder
With jets that stay the course
With talons at the ready
Our U.S. Air Force.

We do salute
Those Neptune's of the ocean
Who have a long tradition
Our U.S. Navy is ready
With ships and ammunition.

We do salute
Those who often go ashore
As a group or as in teams
Their duties are so varied
Our United States Marines.

We do salute
Those who move by tank or feet
Or jump our of planes
They represent our Army
With a multitude of names.

We do salute
Our militia of civilian life
Who wait with sturdy nerves
For the message that we need you
Our national reserves.

We do salute
All who serve and face the flow
Of evil's rising tide
And just like our ancestors
We'll be there by your side.

THE SENTRY WALKED HIS POST

The night was bleak with clouds of gray
And the wind was at its worst
The trees were alive in an eerie sway
As if they had been cursed.
The lights grew dim like heavy eyes
And coldness settled throughout
And even the grass he did surmise
Began to dance about.
Still-the sentry walked his post.

A thunderous roar with flashing lights
A heavy gale it did descend
And the wind with its many frights
Slapped, his face again, and again.
His weapon heavy and his legs were numb
And time had tired his eyes
He knew there'd be no mercy from
The cold and ominous skies.
Still-the sentry walked his post.

A tedious task it was for him
To take each dutiful step
He craved the warmth of houses within
And he cried as he slowly crept.
The night was weakening, yielding to dawn
And the wind was losing its might
But the coldness and rain lingered on
Like companions of the night
Still-the sentry walked his post.

His gait was slower his body in pain
Even his pride was at its ebb
His heart it beat as fast as the rain
And matched the throbbing in his head.

The tortuous elements were at their peak
And so was the soldier sad and distraught
And suddenly his rifle began to reek
And no one heard the single shot
For-the sentry quit walking his post.

They found his form behind a tree
With a smile borne of relief
As if death had set him free
To ease his pain and grief.
They looked inside his pocket
And found a one page letter
That contained a silver locket
Of him in an army sweater.
This-sentry who walked his post.

They slowly read what the letter said
From his girl so far away.
I had to write even though I dread
What I am about to say.
Our time is up and what this means
You must look for someone new
I know it's a shock to end our dreams
But these words are overdue.
For-this sentry who walked his post.

I met a man in the spring
All of it by chance
Now I wear his wedding ring
We have a true romance.
I wish you well, peace and fun
In whatever you may do
I know you'll find that someone
That girl who's right for you.
This sentry who walked his post.

Hardly anyone came to see him
When they laid him down to rest
He had no family or next of kin
This small town in the west.
The girl who sent the letter
Was nowhere to be seen
Perhaps it was for the better
It would have caused a scene.
She was his finest hour
This girl he loved the most
The dreadful stormy day
When-the sentry quit walking his post.

OUR MOMENT IN TIME

This time when I read
The Declaration of Independence,
that paper, that spirit,
which defines who I am,
I closed my eyes
and envisioned our forefathers.
Oh I scanned it before
on national holidays
in the usual perfunctory way.
But this time as I perused
I really felt its meaning.
It is still as relevant
in this maelstrom of modern day.
If you get immersed in the words,
and its intent,
one can't help but pause and reflect
on our nations birth,
and the minutemen,
and those rebellious forefathers,
who cast off the yoke of oppression
vowing to sacrifice to that cause
their lives, their fortune
and their sacred honor.
That allegiance
has been the drum beat of dedication
that has resonated
down through centuries,
which generation after generation
has marched to.
Even when time
indelible stamped that allegiance
Onto my generation,
then continued on.
Time had lifted our adulthood

99

and gently placed it
in the middle of the 20th century.
We were the fortunate ones
to live through war and conflict,
yet, never to fight in any.
In our early youth
we experienced material sacrifice
while our fathers, brothers
and sister wore military uniforms.
And when time
had increased our age,
we too answered the call
and we proudly served our country.
Time
had placed us
in the clam eye
of a cold-war hurricane
and the only fear
we faced was of the unknown.
We never felt the fright of
storming a pacific beachhead.
Nor the horror
of the butchered beaches of Normandy.
And time
had not yet placed us
on the 38th Parallel.
We were nestled
between Korea and Viet Nam
Time
had replaced us
with others to endure
the oppressive jungles of Viet Nam,
or the embassy in Iran,
or Desert Storm,
or other worldwide firestorms.
We witnessed
the fall of the Berlin Wall

and the collapse of Communism,
yet through it all
a calm had passed over our generation
for we were not needed
in any conflict
for time held us in her embrace.
We never looked into terrors face.
We never felt our heartbeat race.
We never aimed our weapons.
We never once did fire.
We never suffered wounds.
We never held a dying comrade.
We never cried our in frustration.
We never cried.
We never saw despair.
We never saw starvation.
We never reveled in victory.
We never received Purple Hearts.
We were never honored in parades.
We were never heroes.
We were never praised.
Still, we would have been
if time had decreed it.
We were always ready
and we did our part.
Time
did require that we serve.
Some of us were assigned to foreign lands,
and there were some
anxious moments,
but they passed without upheaval
and we came back
to the land of the free
and we lived our lives
unencumbered.
We faced only domestic challenges
like employment,

new cars,
and new lives.
I often wondered
why
through all the millenniums
that we were
one of a few American generations
that was blessed with minimal struggles?
It is a question
that bewilders our generation.
But time,
as it has knighted
just a precious few,
gave us a respite
from war and evil.
We were no less American,
no less patriotic
And no less willing to serve.
And in our time in history
we would have pledged
to our God and country
our lives, our fortunes
and our sacred honor.
Now the torch
has been passed beyond our view
to our grandchildren
who know what to do,
and time will lead the way
I will read again
that Declaration
But not just
on Independence day.
I will salute our flag
and our national symbols
and reach out
to the citizens of this land
who firmly believe

and extol those words
that these truths to be self-evident...
that we pledge our lives
our fortunes
and our sacred honor.

OUR FIRST AMENDMENT

It was TV as usual at our retirement home
When they showed some dissenters out to dethrone.
They waved their banners that reeked with despise
Banners of hatred, distrust and lies.
They pulled out our flag as if to amaze
They threw it to the ground then set it ablaze.
Where was this country, this faction of hate
Who took to the streets to infuriate?
Amid this harrow the reporter did say
Where were they from? The USA.
They proclaimed their right to boldly protest
Alas! It was true we couldn't contest
All our amendments they boldly entreat
While ignoring the flag which lay at their feet.
Here in my room I could watch no more
I felt depressed, as if we'd lost a war
I ran to my closet for a plastic bag
A container of memories and my American flag.
My heart embraced it as tears did recall
This gift from a nation for a son who gave all.
Malcontents now desecrate his name
And millions more whose memories remain.
Is our Constitution, like our Universe, expanding?
Beyond interpretation or is it not too demanding?
Then a thought swept over me and it brightened my day
They have the right to tread in their misguided way.
It may be uneasy to comprehend
Their freedom of speech is a right we defend.
It's a tribute to veterans alive or beyond
And to all the patriots who never despond.
To all our countrymen who fought for this day
We only grow stronger when we have our say.
For those who burn a flag or step on a tradition
Hear their precious words, and your own intuition.

Observe their message of antipathy
And shake you head in sympathy.
Feel the irony that warms and delights
As they try to rend our Bill Of Rights
If they libel and slander this hallowed institution
It makes that paper stronger, the US Constitution.

MOUNT RUSHMORE

Fashioned from a dream
Chiseled out of stone
There for all to see
Like men upon a throne.

A monumental treasure
Near our northern door
Four historic men
There on Mount Rushmore.

Borglum had a dream
To make a great impression
And his carvers chiseled on
During the Great Depression.

Each one had excelled
When they were president
Advancing this country
And this continent.

Washington was first
The father of our land
He was joined by Lincoln
The Union it did stand.

Then Jefferson appeared
Who was mighty with the pen
And Theodore Roosevelt
Who forged us on again.

This labor of love
This Shrine of Democracy
Was built to endure
To last through centuries.

If you looking up
When the sun begins to rise
You can't help but notice
The twinkle in their eyes.

These presidential four
Who were meant to endure
Gaze out with satisfaction
That the nation is secure.

WORDS OF OUR ANCESTORS

When my spirit is battered
and I'm overwhelmed with ennui
I escape to the pages of
our American history,
and bathe in the words
of our forefathers
who gave us inspiration.
I marvel at Patrick Henry
orating in St. John's church
to an overflowing crowd
yearning for words of hope.
And from the very depth of his soul
he united them that night
with fiery oration:
"There is no longer any room for hope
If we wish to be free
Is life so dear or peace so sweet
As to be purchased at the price
Of chains and slavery?
Forbid It, Almighty God - I know not what
Course others may take but as for me
Give me liberty or give me death."
Oh his words were like bullets
they penetrated deep.
As deep as Thomas Paine's
an Englishman who took up
the cause of the Revolutionists
his pen thrust forward
in December of 1776.
"These are the times that try men's souls."
His rallying cry that sent
our troops across the Delaware to victory.
That phrase reverberates
in renewed prophecy today.
Often I vicariously go behind enemy lines

with that courageous Connecticut Ranger
Captain Nathan Hale
who, when captured, was stripped of
every civil request
as he faced the hanging tree.
However, his words did escape
to stay the revolution
when he proudly proclaimed
"I regret that I have only one life to give to my country."
And the unflappable John Paul Jones
who informed his enemy
"I have not yet begun to fight."
The father of our country
left us with a treasure chest of inspiration.
From his youth,
to his victorious military days.
And before, during, and after
his term as President.
His first inaugural address was like an anthem
"I was summoned by my country whose voice
I can never hear but with veneration and love"
And the drum beat of devotion
and the heartbeat of patriotism
and the footsteps of love of country
continued on.
Even in that painful period of a divided Union
and of the man who saved it.
He was a beacon of hope
with rays of encouragement.
An orator with a message
whenever he spoke
But none were so memorable
as on the Fall November day
at Gettysburg when
he concluded a short speech with
"Of the people, by the people, for the people
Shall not perish from the earth."
Those words will be read from

Americans yet unborn.
And the pages roll on
generation after generation
From: "Remember the Alamo"
to "Remember The Maine"
To George M's "Over There"
And then came:
"We have nothing to fear but fear itself."
"Give Em Hell Harry."
"Ask not what your country can do for you
But what you can do for your country.'
to: "Mr. Gorbachev - tear down this wall."
And there for all to see is Lady Liberty and to read
"I lift my lamp beside the golden door."
And whether we sing "My country tis of thee,
Sweet Land of Liberty"
Or, "Stand beside her and guide her
through the night with light from above."
Songs or poems, deeds or action
my heart it swells with admiration
of the words of our ancestors
and their indomitable spirit
their quest for adventure
from the engraved writings left
behind in the stones and trees of
our ancestors rolling west.
And one of the greatest moments in
world history
"Tranquillity base the Eagle has landed."
And that breathless moment
the whole world waited to
hear from an American Astronaut named
Neil Armstrong
"That's one small step for a man, one giant leap
for mankind."
And on September 11th in the year 2001
We heard the heroic words of Flight 93
"Let's Roll."

And the words of our leaders today.
"We will bring them to justice
or we will take justice to them"
And those quaking words
Afghanistan is free.
Iraq is free.
We are asked to persevere and one
only has to listen to our anthem
to summon up the will when we sing
"And our flag was still there."
And I feel it most when I try to answer
the question of Abigail Adams the wife
of her husband John and our second president
when she apparently was looking to us,
every American when she asked
and wondered
If future generations will ever realize how
much they suffered
and sacrificed for liberty and freedom.
And from the greatest source of all inspirations
Thomas Jefferson and his Declaration of Independence
When our forefathers swore
"We mutually pledge to each other our Lives, our Fortune
and our sacred Honor.
We still sing out "God Bless America"
and we pledge allegiance to the flag.
The roll call of words is endless
and the pages of the future are
still to be written
but history, thou art an
inspirational companion
and you move my spirit
with pride and humility
and all of us lay claim to
these words
"I am an American."

FACES OF THE FUTURE

I opened up a history book
And there looking up at me
Were these future Americans
Coming from across the sea.

The photo was at least a lifetime
And from it I could surmise
That nothing could stop their quest
I could see it in their eyes.

Somewhere in this mass
Representing our chronology
Was our ancestors, our past
The start of our family tree.

They were nestled on a ship
Waiting for that call
Welcome to this land
Welcome one and all.

I was staring at the fiber
The mosaic of our land
The sinew of our nation
Passed from hand to hand.

This manifest of strangers
Yet I knew everyone
From every foreign nation
Every daughter, every son.

When I touched the photo
I wanted them to know
Whomever you are, wherever you are
Your legacy still does glow.

MY MOTHER'S DIARY

All this time I never knew
Until her words I read
And now I stand before you
To tell you what she said.

I must confess I was remiss
About our family tree.
I didn't care, I didn't search
I was filled with apathy.

Oh sweet Lady with the light
I took it for all granted.
I just assumed it was our right
I reaped but never planted.

In my hand this precious book
I never knew she had.
It's a treasure chest of words
Most are happy, some are sad.

It was deep within a trunk
She kept it out of view
She took her secret with her
When she was ninety-two.

It's worn with age
And tarnished from the sun.
It reveals several days
In nineteen twenty one.

All the pages in this book
Number eighty-two.
And every word she wrote
Defines her love for your.

She scribed of how you came to be
Her quest and inspiration.
That you would light her way
To reach her destination.

Of the tired and of the poor
She knew you'd quell the storm
To all who reached out
To stand before your form.

She wrote of her decision
To cast aside the old.
To leave behind her lineage
And watch the new unfold.

Her decision was traumatic
To uproot and leave a home
With the smallest of a dowry
She was nineteen and alone.

But she saved and toiled all her youth
Morning, noon and night
Until one day she finally sailed
To you, the lady with the light.

Embarking alone with a throng
Burning with the same intent
They all had one way passage
To this giant continent.

Even though she quaked
Upon a rolling sea
She held a picture to her breast
Of you Miss Liberty.

With each wave that moved her on
Heaved with trepidation
But you dear lady carried her will
With great anticipation.

And there it was that teeming shore
Rising with the dawn
Drawing nearer, becoming dearer
And all her doubts were gone.

With a shaky hand she did write
How they all raced to see
Their first glimpse of freedom
This land of Liberty.

When the vessel reached the harbor
And she saw your silhouette
She put these words on paper
This - How can one forget?

And as the ship drew nearer
Her tears began to flow
And she fell to her knees
Beneath your awesome glow.

Her tears they stained the diary
While recording all she saw
Her first view of America
This land of righteous law.

She noticed how the sun
Unveiled a tapestry
Of a nation awakening
As far as the eye could see.

As the ship drew even closer
Your spirit came alive
To all who gazed upon you
Who came here to survive.

Your copper being so erect
With flowing sheaths of green
And that torch above your head
Was a fulfillment to a dream.

She saw that Declaration
Cradled in your hand
And your star like tiara
Upon that head so grand.

She wrote of your gaze
Friendly, but oh so firm
Looking for the homeless
Who had nowhere to turn.

And standing beside you
Flowing in regal manner
Her newly adopted flag
The Star-Spangled Banner.

This was that shining moment
She longed for from the start
And she slowly moved her hand
Upon a trembling heart.

When she stepped on Ellis Island
She kneeled and kissed the ground
This is my land and home
Where freedom does abound.

Her hand raced to pen
From a transcribing mind
The pleasant sights and sounds
One could ever hope to find.

And there she wrote a vow
In nineteen twenty one
That you'll be proud of me
With every setting sun.

She was duly logged and lodged
And there she spent the night
And from a crowded room
She could see your shining light.

On her final page of paper
She made a final note
That once a year she'd visit you
And read you what she wrote.

Like the millions who joined her
On those trips across the sea
She became a model citizen
And raised a family.

We always flew the flag
On every holiday
It was flown for a reason
Meant to honor and obey.

She never ever wavered
When in 1941
A battleship was hit
That claimed her only son.

And once a year, every year
Since 1921
She came back to visit you
To tell you what she's done.

Dear lady she is gone
I think of her every day
About your special bond
Two friends along the way.

Because of her, because of you
And this land of second chances
They came by the millions
To this place where life enhances.

If all who came and had retreated
And gave up in exasperation
Then your flame wouldn't glow
And we'd be a lesser nation.

But they ignored the lightning
Of every creed and name
They had that determination
To stand beneath your flame.

So here I stand a mendicant
One who beseeches
Now through my mother's eyes
My spirit it breeches

Now once a year, every year
It's now my legacy
I'll come to you and read to you
My mother's diary.

A PATIENT AND A PROMISE

I'll never forget my 20th birthday
nor the message he left with me.
He was just a simple soldier
dying in a veterans hospital,
not of wounds
but from a broken heart.
Old Eddie was someone special.
He was on the ward the longest
and he always had a smile.
He always was so thankful
The Lord would let him stay awhile.
He never drew attention
to his own incurable malady.
He always comforted others
and told soothing lies,
that all would be well.
He had no wife to comfort him
No children to give him glee,
no relatives to make him laugh,
no friends that I could see.
It seemed the only family
that even seemed to care
were the staff
who knew him
and his peers around the ward.
I'm just a volunteer.
I help wherever I can.
I read to them and
listen to their stories
and it lifts you to tears
that all these men
who lie here
all from different times,
all who sacrificed something,

for this country they call home.
I give my time
for many reasons,
mainly for my dad,
who's missing in Vietnam.
He was all I ever had
mom died when I was three.
It's the least that I could do
he taught me very well.
He said always be a man
be gentle but be firm,
be truthful to yourself,
to respect another point of view,
and always salute the flag,
and remember where you're from.
On this special day
I had something to share
And the patients on the ward
were eager to hear
that I had joined the army
and this was my last day.
They even made a cake for me,
from the patients and the staff,
all the cards they gave me
are still home in a drawer.
I had to say good-bye to them
It would surely break my heart.
I shook their hands,
one by one,
it tore me all apart.
And then I came to Eddie
lying in his room.
The heavy medication
was holding on to life.
He knew the Lord was coming,
coming to call him home
but he wanted a word with me.

It meant a lot to him.
He thanked me for all I'd done
and wished me a happy birthday.
And with painful tears
he said to me
I'm the son he never had.
I put my arm around him
and said you'd be a great dad.
Then he asked
if I would make a promise
that would please him
and my father very much.
I couldn't refuse
not when he evoked my dad's name.
So with a heavy heart I took his hand
and asked what he wished.
Son, he said I'm going say
things I never told anyone
because I never had anyone
to tell them to.
And that is important.
In many ways I've been a fool
I wasted all my youth,
and even in my later years
that too was of no use.
And before I knew it
there were no longer
youthful tomorrow's,
or uncharted adventures,
or a hand to hold in mine.
Go enjoy your youth
explore the world
and seek out new careers
but always remember
who you are and
where you are from.
It was if dad

was before me again.
Struggling to continue he added,
Life is the most precious thing on earth.
It is a stream
that must be shared,
but not soiled.
Remember to pursue your dreams
no matter how insurmountable.
To persevere
and never submit to failure.
And don't bathe in the words
what might have been.
And consider this,
life is to be shared.
Be cautious
but not cynical.
Grasp the hand of a loved one
and hold on through life,
for it all ends so soon, too soon.
And if you lead a life like me
you go to your grave
with a mountain of regrets
and a trunk full of "what ifs"
and loneliness.
I have mistaken companionship
for friendship.
I have mistaken love
for infatuation.
I have mistaken commitment
for entanglement.
I have mistaken family
for impediments.
Now it comes down to this
a lonely room
and an empty chair.
Remember me,
but more importantly

remember yourself,
And heed the words
of and old soldier.
With his words penetrating my heart
I hugged him
and wished him well
and promised
that I would strive to
achieve his words of wisdom
and I clasped his hand
than walked away.
I received a letter
from one of the ward nurses
telling me that
Old Eddie passed away a week later.
He was given a full military funeral
and no one was there
except the local veterans organization.
I cried when I read the letter,
Especially the words…
no one was there.
Night was descending at our base
And they began to play retreat
as they lowered the flag
with a bugle's horn
and tears streaming
down unashamedly
I stood up and saluted
Old Eddie and my dad
And I'll never forget
where I'm from.
For I have promises to keep.

RUM, TRINKETS AND GRAVES

High atop a mountain
an Indian Warrior rides
And pulls his pinto to a halt
And gazes at the sky.

Then stares down at the valley
There for all to see
The transformation of nature
A refuse of humanity.

Where once the air was pure
Where the waters would roam
Where the salmon and the hawk
Knew this was their home.

Where once all of his ancestors
Purified the land
By praying to that spirit
Who created earth and man.

For centuries they hunted
They valued all its worth
They praised all of nature
The sun, the moon, the earth.

Then the dream was shattered
Blown by all the winds
When the white man came ashore
With their unforgiving sins.

Eventually the tribes
Began to go asunder
Giving up their lands
To white man's thunder.

All of their land
From one sea to the other
By hand or by deceit
Was taken from each brother.

All of their treaties
Useless and absurd
They learned to be cautious
Of the white man at his word.

Chief Tecumseh knew
When he spoke to his braves
We gave them land with game
For rum, trinkets, and graves.

Every act, every word
A past that came to be
The Trail of Tears, the massacres
The blood at Wounded Knee.

Disease, famine, war
Companions among the throng
They have claimed the lives
Of ten million strong.

Their names are etched in memory
Of shamans and story tellers
Of riders of the plains
Of forests, and cliff dwellers.

The Iroquois, Mohawk,
Ottawa, Pawnee
Delaware, Fox
Peoria, Shawnee.

Pequot, Kaw
Seneca, Ute
Mohegan, Oneida,
Hopi, Paiute

Tuscarora, Sioux
Mandan, Arapaho
Chumsahs, Pomo
Ponca, Navaho.

Onodaga, Cheyenne
Pueblo, Omaha.
Sauk, Miami
Apache, Wichita.

Kickapoo, Creek
Pomo, Chippawa.
Seminole, Mohave
Alabama, Chickasaw.

Arikara, Winnebago
Naticoke, Comanche
Iowa, Chitamacha
Shoshone, Cherokee

The scroll is endless
It reaches to the sky
The Walla, Walla, Modoc
Shinnecock and I.

Now all of us are shadows
Of how it used to be
The bottle and the drugs
Are current maladies.

But though we're few in number
We still have our stride.
Our will remains strong
Against pernicious genocide

While we may not ride on horses
And no longer throw the spear
We still are making history
Each and every year.

Despite our bold mistreatment
And lies from pen and talk
We know we still belong
With the salmon and the hawk.

MY BUDDY POPPY

It wasn't long ago
When our nation was unfolding
In its unassuming way,
I was safe at home
Aloof to foreign lands
Not caring yea or nay.

I was one amid the crowd
Flowing like a leaf
In a river to the sea.
A stream of nameless faces
I looked at no one,
And no one looked at me.

As I flowed along this river
Braving all the rapids
Of the traffic and the din,
I saw a man
There on the corner
Holding poppies and a tin.

My gaze was on his uniform
His military cap
And a poppy in his lapel.
He was pleading for alms
To give added comfort
For those who fought in hell.

This proud American veteran
Had a smile for everyone
With those poppies in his hand.
I tacitly acknowledged him
Continued down the river
And put nothing in his can.

The only thing I offered
Was pity and dismay
As I raced along with verve.
Oh, I was thankful,
Thankful not to him
But that I never had to serve.

And then that day
That dreadful day
We saw the face of mania.
Crashing into towers,
The Pentagon,
A field in Pennsylvania.

Our change was sudden
As we rose from our knees
And wiped away our awe.
We vowed to track them down
With a military pursuit
And the mighty hand of law.

Again our youth are summoned
To give us pause
Concerning life and war.
Can we stay the course
To apprehend those
Who came knocking at our door?

Then they started coming home
In wheelchairs and in casts,
These the resolute.
Some came home in silence
In coffins draped with flags
With a 21-gun salute.

Now every time I see reports
Of our military under fire
I'm filled with introspection.
They're fighting for freedom
Fighting for peace,
Fighting for my protection.

Often I reflect
Upon this nation's aura
And how it use to be.
We, I, and most of you
Continued on
Like a river to the sea.

How did I come to be
In modern day America
With no patriotic past?
But there is today
And there is tomorrow
To rekindle and recast.

Now whenever I'm in a throng
I stop to look at life
Especially at faces.
I often leave the river
To proudly gaze around
To all that life embraces.

Especially to that man
Standing on a corner
With a tin can in his hand.
Holding all those poppies
Those red buddy poppies
Which represent this land.

They revere the poem of John McCrae
Written in World War One
So many years ago.
In Flanders Field the poppies blow
Between the crosses
Row on Row.

When the vets of foreign wars
Sacrifice their time
For this patriotic plea.
I buy poppies on that corner,
Near that rushing river,
And I'm as content as I can be.

KNOWN BUT TO GOD

Peace, victory, valor
and known but to God.
You and your brethren
are the proud epitome of
a glorious epitaph.
You share an ignoble fate
the consequences of a noble deed.
We know not who you are
nor the soil of freedom
you thread on as a youth.
You left no will just a legacy.
We know of your deeds,
we recorded them
and etched them in our hearts
and on memorials.
You, are among battalions of heroes
who tread on battlefields,
who encountered foes with valor,
who fought for peace,
who assured victory.
You rest with honor,
among interment flags
near your comrades,
representing the unknowns
of those other combat
conflicts of the 20th century.
We salute and mourn you
whomever you are.
You, who represent those
who unceremoniously share your fate.
We, all of us, bear the pleasant yoke
of your inscribed baton-freedom.
Here on this hill at Arlington,
amid the sorrow and the glory,

overlooking a sea of graves
with names, ranks and identity,
you, and your fellow Americans lie
known but to God,
yet honored by all.
Sleep in peace unknown,
you rest without a name save one,
the noblest of all names,
American.

Printed in the United States
1326900003B/103-336